This Notebook Belongs to:

76949892R00058

Made in the USA
San Bernardino, CA
17 May 2018